Community Places

School

by Amy McDonald

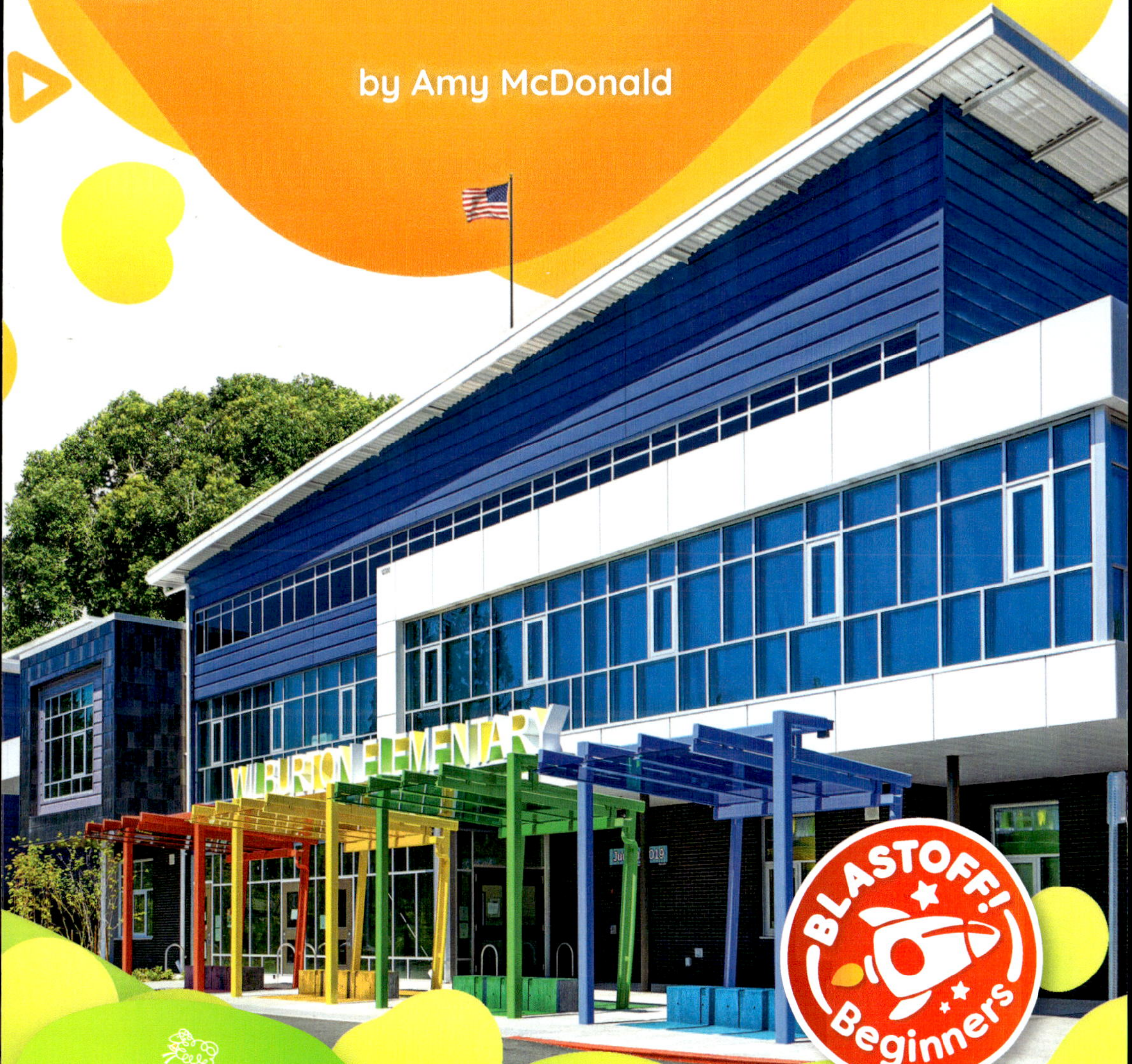

Blastoff! Beginners

BELLWETHER MEDIA
MINNEAPOLIS, MN

Blastoff! Beginners are developed by literacy experts and educators to meet the needs of early readers. These engaging informational texts support young children as they begin reading about their world. Through simple language and high frequency words paired with crisp, colorful photos, Blastoff! Beginners launch young readers into the universe of independent reading.

Sight Words in This Book

and	for	is	so
are	get	it	the
at	have	new	they
day	help	on	time
each	here	play	too
eat	in	run	we

This edition first published in 2022 by Bellwether Media, Inc.

Library of Congress Cataloging-in-Publication Data

LC record for School available at: https://lccn.loc.gov/2021044258

Editor: Christina Leaf Designer: Andrea Schneider

Printed in the United States of America, North Mankato, MN.

Table of Contents

At School!

We are here!
It is time
for school!

What Are Schools?

Schools are busy places. Teachers help students learn.

The School Day

Students learn in classrooms. They read and write at desks.

classroom

They sing
in the music room.
They play
instruments.

music
room

Students eat in the **cafeteria**. They have **healthy** lunches.

healthy lunch

cafeteria

Students read in the library. They get new books.

library

Students run
in the gym.
They play games.

gym

They play on the playground, too. Time for **recess**!

playground

School is fun! We learn so much each day!

School Facts

Inside a School

What Happens in a School?

learn

sing

eat

Glossary

cafeteria

lunchroom

healthy

good for your body

instruments

tools for making music

recess

a play break

To Learn More

ON THE WEB

FACTSURFER

Factsurfer.com gives you a safe, fun way to find more information.

1. Go to www.factsurfer.com.
2. Enter "school" into the search box and click 🔍.
3. Select your book cover to see a list of related content.

Index

The images in this book are reproduced through the courtesy of: knelson20, front cover; Andrew Angelov, p. 3; 2xSamara.com, p. 4; SDI Productions, pp. 4-5, 20-21; Blaj Gabriel, p. 6; Monkey Business Images, pp. 6-7, 8-9; Slatan, p. 8; sunabesyou, p. 10; skynesher, pp. 10-11; Pixel-Shot, p. 12; SolStock, pp. 12-13; Kiryakova Anna, p. 14; wavebreakmedia, pp. 14-15, 23 (instruments); FatCamera, pp. 16-17; Vitaliy Karimov, pp. 18-19; Dean Drobot, p. 20; paulaphoto, p. 22 (inside); Weedezign, p. 22 (learn); Africa Studio, p. 22 (sing); Pressmaster, p. 22 (eat); Monkey Business Images Ltd, p. 23 (cafeteria); Yulia Davidovich, p. 23 (healthy); FamVeld, p. 23 (recess).